One In A Trillion Women Screenplay

Yvonne Stewart-Williams

All rights reserved, no part of this publication may be reproduced by any means, electronic, mechanical photocopying, documentary, film or in any other format without prior written permission of the publisher.

>Published by
>Chipmunkapublishing
>United Kingdom

http://www.chipmunkapublishing.com

Copyright © Yvonne Stewart-Williams 2025

ONE IN A TRILLION WOMAN
Written by
Yvonne Patricia Stewart-Williams
Based on, If Any

Yvonne Stewart-Williams

INT. BEDROOM - DAY 1 FRIDAY

It's morning. A lone woman is lying fully dressed on her locked ward psychiatric hospital bed, with an open laptop nearby. She is sobbing uncontrollably. She remonstrates.

YVONNE

Why? I just want to die.
The mobile phone rings, then stops. Text
sounds can be heard.
Then the phone rings again and is answered.

YVONNE (CONT'D)
Hello

JULIAN
Why haven't you been answering
Yvonne?

YVONNE
Julian, I just want to die.

JULIAN
I'm in court and I want you to
correspond with me Yvonne, Please.
The phone goes dead and text sounds start in
the bedroom.
Yvonne holds the mobile in her hand and
reads the text
message.

JULIAN (CONT'D)
Yvonne I'm getting married to a man
and I am inviting you to the
wedding.

YVONNE
I won't be there Julian.

JULIAN
Why?
There is a pregnant pause.

JULIAN (CONT'D)
Yvonne, why are you not responding?

YVONNE
Julian I'm in love with you and I want you to marry me.

JULIAN
Yvonne we talked through this already. You and I are not lovers; we are best friends.

YVONNE
No Julian, please. This is too hard for me. I can't cope. I want to be your wife. I won't accept you marrying anyone else, especially a man!

JULIAN
Yvonne, please don't be disrespectful. You're not the only one who is hurting. You're my best friend, but I have known him longer than we have known each other. He can't shower me with gifts like you do, but he loves me for me, and has remained celibate for a long time respectfully waiting for me to love him back.

YVONNE
Julian I'm not well. I have been signed off work by the doctor. I am in hospital because I feel suicidal and want to die. The medics want to monitor me.

JULIAN
I'm so sorry to hear that Yvonne. Why do you feel suicidal and want to die?

YVONNE
Because you told me that you don't want me Julian. I can't live with that truth and I can't live without you.

JULIAN
Yvonne, I told you that you are my best friend and I love you and would die for you. But my future husband accepts me for who I am. Come to my wedding and meet him; I love him. You will love him too. I have told him about you.

YVONNE
Julian, I can't lie. I'm pissed that you have chosen to marry a man! Does he know that we were lovers?

> Just then, there is a sound of movement beyond the room door
> and the shouted words of 'Breakfast Time!' Can be heard.

YVONNE (CONT'D)
Julian, I have to go, it's Breakfast time. I'll contact you when I'm done.

JULIAN
Okay, Bye

INT. LOUNGE - DAY 1 FRIDAY

Yvonne puts her mobile down and exits her room and makes her way down the corridor and through the lounge, towards the dining room. Just then a female patient approaches her wearing a nightie and stops her in her tracks. The patient smiles at Yvonne and Yvonne smiles back. Then without speaking or an explanation; the woman reaches out and unexpectedly caresses Yvonne's breasts. Yvonne is shocked and frightened. Yvonne hastily backs away from the woman.

YVONNE
Help! Nurse! Please help me! I have just been fondled by this woman! The impertinence! It's an outrage!

NURSE
What's going on?

YVONNE
This woman has unexpectedly just groped my breasts!
The nurse sighed, then gave Yvonne a knowing sympathetic look.

NURSE
Nobody's perfect.
Yvonne is furious! Outraged. Disgusted. Yvonne stares menacingly at the woman patient and shouts

YVONNE
How dear you fondle my breasts? It's a liberty!
(MORE)

The female patient as if mute, smiles at Yvonne then walks away showing off her exposed bottom through the split of her nightie.
After breakfast Yvonne was given the options of participating in a Art class, a Kundalini Yoga Class or use of the IT Suite. Yvonne chose the latter.

INT. IT SUITE
Yvonne collected her Apple laptop from her room and quickly made her way to the very popular staff facilitated IT Suite. There Yvonne found herself sandwiched in between two patients. Yvonne placed her laptop down in the empty space between two windows computers being used by patients. One patient was wearing headphones and watching YouTube music videos and the other patient was being tutored by a Peer Mentor through the process of creating a email address and a blog. Yvonne discovered that she was still logged into the hospital's free wifi, and found a new lease of energy to surf the web. She then checked her twitter, facebook accounts and created a GarageBand 'Spoken Word' Podcast, which covered the
topic of her hospital stay, which she then uploaded to her 'Soundcloud' account. Throughout there was background chatter
and the odd few words sung from the patient listening to the music videos. Yvonne's twitter and facebook feed informed her that today 1st December was World's AIDS Day. Yvonne remained
stoic.

INT. BEDROOM - DAY 2 - SATURDAY

Yvonne had silenced her phone, since yesterday's incident with the patient and the World AIDS Day reminder. Yvonne had
seen the screen glowing intermittently with Julian's persistent call/texts. Yvonne was in a pensive mood but as it approached lunchtime, she relents and answers the call/texts. Yvonne communicates to Julian about her encounter with the woman yesterday.

YVONNE
What are you going to do about it?

JULIAN
Yvonne, there is nothing that I can do about your mix-up with a woman. Just know that if you do pursue it;

JULIAN (CONT'D)
you can forget about me. God doesn't welcome lesbians

YVONNE
I feel so soiled, Julian! Cheap and sullied! Exploited by both her and YOU! I'm vulnerable. You both took advantage of my womanhood. That patient violated me and sexually abused me and you used me. It was World's AIDS Day, yesterday and I sincerely hope that you are using condoms! I still really love you and I'd be devastated and beside myself with grief, if you became HIV infected. I wanted you to make a honest woman out of me, for you and I to chose our wedding rings together and for us to get married and have children. I envisioned a traditional Quaker Wedding for us. Although I wouldn't have taken your surname, I would have been so proud to be your wife; I still would be!

I visualized you and me being known as one of the most romantic monogamous married couples, and giving each other loads of respect and cuddles. Kissing and massaging my pregnant stomach, accompanying me to anti-natal classes, being by my side and holding my hand during my labour and the birth of our newborn child, and you registering her or his birth. Your surname as well as mine would have been on our child's birth certificate. Although one thing that I would have insisted on, is that our child would of had a double barrelled surname.

JULIAN
Yvonne you're not the only one that's hurting. It's not going to be easy for me to marry a man. Do you want me to leave you alone?

YVONNE
No.

JULIAN
Let's Change the subject.

YVONNE
Okay

JULIAN
Yesterday you asked me if my man knew that we were lovers.

YVONNE
That's right.

JULIAN
No. That would terrify him. He knows that we are best friends; but nothing more than that. You and I grew apart. He and I were in the brotherhood together, shared the same faith with Godly values, plus we were also best friends; but our love just grew deeper and deeper as you and I grew apart. He didn't reveal his feelings for me out of respect for my long term marriage, especially as there were children involved, and he stayed celibate and waited. He didn't disclose how he really felt about me until I told him that my marriage was acrimonious and irreconcilable.

YVONNE
Do you remember our first kiss?

JULIAN
I'm trying hard to forget.

YVONNE
Julian, I'm still in love with you. Please can we be lovers after your wedding?

JULIAN
No! Certainly not. Why, just because I'm marrying a man? You wouldn't like it if you were to marry and I insisted on being your lover after your wedding! Would You?

YVONNE
No, definitely not!
(MORE)

JULIAN
Okay.

YVONNE
Julian, please don't think less of me, for trying to get you back, after all I have loved you for years. I know that you're one of the most devoutly God fearing, and law abiding individuals. You; in fact your whole family are active members of your church, and are present there every week. I would never have imagined for one minute, that you would have got involved in a gay relationship in such a homophobic society, and now, I hate the idea of your intention to marry a man. Please, marry me instead.

JULIAN
Yvonne we've talked about this already.

YVONNE
Julian, I want to ask you a question, but please don't be mad with me.

JULIAN
Go Ahead.

YVONNE
I love you. Do you love me?

JULIAN
I love you Yvonne.

YVONNE
Then marry me.

JULIAN
I have said no so many times. We

are best friends. I know that I would be alright with you materially and that you would take care of me okay, but I no longer want to marry a woman. My man, loves me for me and respects me, and I love him for that, and intend to marry him.
JULIAN (CONT'D)
(MORE)

He doesn't have money to shower me with gifts like you do, but I know he will love and cherish me for the rest of my life.
Just then, a voice could be heard beyond the door calling out
'Last Chance to get lunch!'. Yvonne stopped texting, exited her room and made her way to the dining room. On arrival, Yvonne found herself at the end of a long queue with restless, hungry, angry, riotous impatient psychiatric inpatients; surrounded by staff. There is a delay at the front of the queue, because a patient has been refused sticky toffee pudding, due to her obesity.

PATIENT
I'm here for my mental health, not my physical health. If I want a sticky toffee pudding, I can have it!
Things spiral out of control and a riot ensues with shouting and banging, barging and pushing. The staff close the hatch to the kitchen and escort the patients from the dining room.

A bewildered and shaken Yvonne leaves the dining room without lunch.

INT. CHAPEL - DAY 3 - SUNDAY

Yvonne sits patiently in the pews of the chapel waiting for the service to begin. She glances at the hymn books and religious regalia and thinks to herself that this is so dissimilar to her simple Quaker Meetings for Worship, where she enjoys the role of being an Overseer with Pastoral Care for her local Friends Meeting House. The hospital chapel is nearly empty. Seated beside her are two similarly dressed older Jamaican women, who are fussing over each other and holding hands. They introduce themselves to her as a Seventh Day Adventist married couple. Yvonne recognizes one of the spouses, as the patient on her locked ward who caused yesterday's near riot, over the sticky toffee pudding. The woman whispers to Yvonne in hushed tones, while looking lovingly at her partner.

S/T/P WOMAN
```
She was a man, when we first got
married, many years ago, one
Sabbath in the midst of our local
Seventh Day Adventist faith based
congregation, home group.
```

S/T/P WOMAN (CONT'D)

```
Then after we had the children, she
had the operation. Now we are a
happily married lesbian couple. We
remain cemented in our faith with
God; and we are both well loved,
respected and greatly appreciated
Sisters within our local Sabbath
School and community. We never miss
Service on a Sabbath; except when I
am an inpatient, and then we visit
this chapel on a Sunday instead. We
are devoted to each other. I love
her so much. More and more
everyday. I feel so blessed to have
her in my life, and I couldn't ask
for a better marriage partner,
```

faithful companion and friend. For
better or worse and in sickness and
health. Not only do we share all
each others clothes. We also share
all the chores.

INT. CONSULTANCY ROOM - DAY 4 - MONDAY

Yvonne sat looking out of the window as the psychiatrist probes Yvonne's relationship with her ex-husband.

PSYCHIATRIST
I see from your records that you don't have any children and that you are divorced and the instigator of the divorce.

YVONNE
Yes.

PSYCHIATRIST
I can also see from your records that you divorced your ex-husband because you claimed that he was 'gay'.

YVONNE
That's correct.

PSYCHIATRIST
That you became depressed, self medicated on alcohol and drugs then experienced a psychotic episode, became paranoid and was hospitalized.

YVONNE
Yes! But that was then, this is now. Why are you talking about my ex-husband?

PSYCHIATRIST
Because you appear to attract latent homosexuals.

YVONNE
Hmmmm

PSYCHIATRIST
Yvonne, you have experienced a relationship breakdown. I'm going to sign you off work for three week. Pursue some hobbies, meet with your family and friends. Take a short holiday. Who knows, perhaps you'll meet a man who can return your love.
Just then it dawned on Yvonne, why her relationship with
Julian drifted apart.

YVONNE
Doctor, I have just realized that I am a lesbian. I have been in the closet and hiding for some time and been nervous to come out. You have helped me to be real and honest with myself.

PSYCHIATRIST
So, no more Julian?

YVONNE
I will always love Julian; no matter what. She is my very best friend.

PSYCHIATRIST
Are you telling me that Julian is a woman?

YVONNE
Yes, doctor. Julian is a Woman.

Yvonne Stewart-Williams

www.ingramcontent.com/pod-product-compliance
Lightning Source LLC
Chambersburg PA
CBHW040301170426
43193CB00020B/2968